W9-ANE-988

	DATE DUE		

Farm Animals

Children's Nature Library

HTS BOOKS
AN IMPRINT OF FOREST HOUSE™
School & Library Edition

87654321
ISBN 0-88176-145-1

Written by Eileen Spinelli

Credits:
Animals/Animals: 36, 64; Mike Andrews, 48;
Henry Ausloos, 34, 60; Miriam Austerman, 18;
Norvia Behing, 26; G. I. Bernard, 4, 18, 20, 26;
George R. Cassidy, 40; Ken Cole, 31; Margot
Conte, 17, 20, 44; Jerry Cooke, 30, 44, 50; Harry
Cutting, 42; Stephen Dalton, 60; E. R. Degginger,
7, 12, 16, 28, 40, 43, 52, 55, 62; Adrienne T.
Gibson, 14; Geo. F. Godfrey, 12, 14, 28; Gary W.
Griffen, 34, 53; Marcia W. Griffen, 8; Mike &
Elvan Habicht, 40, 58; S. D. Halperin, 28; R. F.
Head, 34; Holt Studio Ltd., 9, 10, 33, 54, 59;
Susan Jones, 6, 48; Breck P. Kent, 8, 40, 61;
Richard Kolar, 46, 47, 56, 58; Leporidae, 27; Zig
Leszczynski, 26, 46, 48; Ken Lewis, 41; Robert
Maier, 21, 23, 38, 45, 52, 57, 63, Bruce A.
McDonald, 62; Joe & Carol McDonald, 50; Roger
B. Minkoff, 32; Wendy Neefus, 13, 32, 56;
Oxford Scientific, 20; Charles Palek, 10, 12, 42, 46;
Robert Pearcy, Front Cover, 1, 38; John L. Pontier,
14, 18, 19; Fritz Prenzel, 20, 35, 36; Maresa Pryor,
30, 52; Michael & Barbara Reed, 37; Ralph A.
Reinhold, Back Cover, 11, 24, 29, 39, 51, 58;
L. L. T. Rhodes, 16; Ray Richardson, 24; C. W.
Schwartz, 25, 60, 62; Donald Specker, 3, 15, 22, 28;
J. C. Stevenson, 16, 48; A. Thomas, 42; David
Thompson, 34; Sydney Thomson, 50; Jim Tuten,
62; Doug Wechsler, 22; Fred Whitehead, 49;
Harold E. Wilson, 24; **Earth Scenes:** E. R.
Degginger, 5; Breck P. Kent, 6; Zig Leszczynski,
4; **Gerry Ellis Wildlife:** 54.

Table of Contents

Introduction

Long ago there were no farms. People searched for berries and roots and hunted for meat. About ten thousand years ago, people began to plant the seeds of wild plants so they would have a supply of vegetables, fruit, and grain.

Their crops attracted hungry wild animals. Sheep and goats came to eat in the gardens, and people decided to tame them. This gave them a steady supply of meat and also milk. Raising animals was less trouble than hunting.

Introduction

Throughout the world there are many different kinds of farm animals. In some places, reindeer are raised on farms. In other places, elephants, camels, and llamas do farm work.

Most farms now use tractors and other large machines to plow fields and harvest crops. But there is still work on the farm for horses, donkeys, dogs, cats, and even geese, as you will find out in this book.

Some farms raise only one kind of animal. There are pig farms, chicken farms, and turkey farms. Other farms keep many kinds of animals. You'll learn about these animals when you read this book.

Sheep

Sheep are the first kind of animal that people raised on farms. Long ago, farmers kept sheep only for their milk. Later, people began to use their warm coats for clothing. Sheep are also used for meat.

Ram

Ewes

A female sheep is called a ewe. A male sheep is a ram. Their babies are lambs. Sheep live in flocks. If a sheep is taken out of the flock, it gets upset. Because they like to stick together, sheep look like they are playing follow the leader. They often follow the oldest ewe wherever she goes. Sheep also follow specially trained sheepdogs.

Sheep eat hay, cornstalks, weeds, shrubs, and grass. They will not drink from running water, so the farmer must fill a drinking trough for them.

Lamb

8

Sheep

Shearing a sheep with electric shears

Sheared sheep

A sheep's fur is called wool. Every spring, a sheep gets a haircut. This is called shearing. A skilled person carefully shears the sheep. The wool is then cleaned and spun into yarn to make cloth.

Sheep are gentle and playful. They make good pets. They also make good lawn mowers.

Goats

The milk you drink probably comes from a cow. But in many parts of the world, people drink goat's milk. It is also used to make many kinds of cheese and delicious butter.

Female goats are called nanny goats. They are about the same size as large sheep. Male goats are billy goats. They are about the same size as small ponies. Babies are kids. When they are newborn, they're about as large as house cats.

Goats

Goats are acrobatic. They jump and leap, and can even climb trees. They like to butt their horns. When a goat meets a friend, they butt heads to say hello. Goats also butt each other in pretend fights. If you let a goat get behind you, it may butt you.

Goats eat almost everything. They eat oats and hay, but they also eat gloves, string, paper, and glue. They do not eat tin cans.

Ducks

Many farmers used to raise ducks for their eggs. But today farmers keep ducks mostly for meat and feathers. Ducks also help the farmer by eating insects and grubs that harm crops.

On land, ducks waddle on their short legs and webbed feet. In the water, they swim easily and gracefully. Their feathers are waterproof, so they can stay in water for a long time.

A mother duck doesn't know her babies by sight. But she does know their voices. If a duckling is lost or frightened, all it has to do is quack, and mother duck comes running.

Chickens

People have been raising chickens for thousands of years. In ancient Greece, even people who lived in the city kept chickens. When the Spanish explorers and the Pilgrims came to North and South America, they brought chickens with them from Europe.

Female chickens are called hens. On small farms, hens make their nests in chicken coops. The farmer collects their eggs in a basket. On large farms, hens are kept in cages. Their eggs are collected on a moving belt as they are laid. One hen lays about 240 eggs each year.

Male chickens are called roosters. They do not lay eggs, and they do not help raise the chicks. Most people know that roosters crow in the morning and wake up the farmer. But roosters also crow in the late afternoon.

Chickens

Baby chickens work very hard to peck their way out of their shells. When a chick finally makes it out, it is tired and wet. Within a few hours, the chick is dry and lively, and covered with white or yellow fluff.

Chicks must stay warm for the first three weeks of their lives. The farmer keeps them indoors. When they are ready to go out, they run happily around the chicken yard. At night or if there is danger, mother hen gathers her chicks under her wing.

Geese

There are two kinds of geese on the farm. Wild geese come to the pond in the spring and fall. Domestic geese live on the farm all year. Farmers raise geese for their feathers, which are used to make soft down pillows and comforters.

Geese live in families. Father and mother goose work together to make a nest. Then they both sit on the eggs and take care of the babies.

Geese

Did you know that geese make good watchdogs? Geese are very noisy. When they are surprised, they honk loudly. It is almost impossible to sneak up on a flock of geese.

Farm geese eat dried corn, greens, and grass. Unlike wild geese they can't fly. They are too heavy to get off the ground.

Rabbits

Many rabbits that live on farms are pets, but some farmers raise rabbits for their meat and fur.

Rabbits don't just like to eat carrots. They like peanuts and a lot of other foods. Rabbits need to gnaw on wood. This keeps their teeth from growing too long.

Rabbits are usually very quiet. But when there is danger, they use their back feet to thump out a warning.

If you ever pick up a rabbit, lift it by the scruff of the neck. Picking it up by the ears hurts the rabbit.

Cattle

Cattle come in many colors: red, black, tan, and white. Some have patterned coats. Farmers raise beef cattle for meat and dairy cattle for milk.

Dairy cattle usually weigh a lot less than beef cattle. On small farms, the farmer milks the cows by hand. On large farms, cows are milked by machine.

Cattle

Male cattle are called bulls. They are large, strong animals. Farmers build strong pens for bulls. Sometimes the farmer puts a ring in a bull's nose to make him easier to handle.

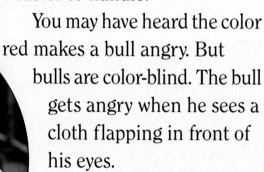

You may have heard the color red makes a bull angry. But bulls are color-blind. The bull gets angry when he sees a cloth flapping in front of his eyes.

Cattle

Some scientists believe that cattle almost never sleep. They spend half their time lying down in the shade. The rest of the time they graze. When the weather is warm, cattle even graze at night.

Cattle

Some farmers stay in the barn with the cow while she is giving birth to a calf. When her baby is born, the farmer helps mother cow clean it and keep it warm.

The newborn calf is weak and tired at first. It needs to rest for about an hour, then it wobbles to its feet. If it is a warm day, mother cow takes her baby outside. If it is cold, they stay in the barn.

Dogs

Border collie

Most dogs who live on the farm have their own jobs to do. Collies are hardworking sheepdogs. They guide sheep to their pen. That's the easy part. Then the dog has to get the sheep to go into the pen.

Corgis help the farmer take care of the cattle. They take cattle from the barn to pasture. The dog keeps the herd moving by nipping at the legs of the slower cows.

36

Dogs

Fox terriers

Terriers help farmers bring in the cows at milking time. They also hunt rats and mice in the barn. A terrier is a good watchdog, and so is a German shepherd.

German shepherd

Horses

Horses do heavy work on the farm. The pioneers who settled the United States used horses to clear the land and plow their fields. Today, farm horses pull wagons. In Vermont, horses pull sleds loaded with maple sap to the sugar house where it is made into syrup. Even on large farms with big machinery, horses are kept for riding and recreation.

Horses

Quarter horse

Different kinds of horses do different kinds of farm work. Cowboys ride quarter horses when they round up cattle. This kind of horse is also used to haul logs.

The English shire is the heaviest kind of horse. It can weigh a ton. On a tree farm, it hauls trees to the mill. On a ranch, it pulls wagons loaded with hay.

English shire

Horses

Morgan

The Morgan is a fast runner and often wins races. But on the farm, a Morgan pulls the hay wagon.

The Clydesdale is a good worker. It is strong and sturdy. It does all its farm chores with high-stepping energy.

44

Horses

Horses like to graze on grass. They also eat hay, oats, corn, and bran. Carrots and apples are their favorite treats.

A horse sleeps for several hours each day. But each nap is very short. Horses sleep standing up most of the time. They like a soft bed of hay, straw, or wood shavings if they can get one.

Donkeys

Donkeys have many jobs on the farm. They can pull plows or carry crops to market. Shepherds ride donkeys, and ranchers use donkeys to calm wild young horses.

A donkey eats wheat, barley, oats, hay, and vegetables. Its favorite treat is cake. But a donkey will refuse to drink stale water.

Donkeys cost less than horses. They work longer hours, and they eat less than horses. Donkeys are patient and friendly, but they are easily bored. You have to keep your donkey busy or play with it. If you don't, the donkey may chew a big hole in the barn just to have something to do.

Cats

Do you know what a farm cat does? It catches mice and rats that steal grain from the barn.

Some farm cats aren't as friendly as house cats. They will not even stand still long enough to be petted.

Cats like to run in the fields. They like to take catnaps in the sun. At milking time, farm cats gather in the barn hoping to get a dish of fresh milk.

Turkeys

Many farmers used to keep small flocks of turkeys. But now most turkeys are raised on big farms.
On the turkey farm, the birds move around outside. If the sun gets too hot or if it starts to rain, the turkeys can go under nearby sheds. Turkeys get sick easily. Farmers who keep turkeys must watch over their flocks very carefully.

Pigs

Do you know why pigs like to play in mud puddles? It's not because they like to get dirty. Pigs are one of the cleanest animals on the farm. They take mud baths to keep cool.

Pigs are also one of the smartest animals. A pig can be taught to do tricks, just like a dog.

Pigs

On some farms, pigs find their own food. They are sent out into the fields and forests to dig in the earth for their dinner. But on most farms, pigs are fed by the farmer. They eat grain, milk, and table scraps. If they are lucky, they may be given stale donuts for dessert. The only things pigs don't like to eat are onions and tomatoes.

Have you heard someone say that a person who eats too much is a pig? That person doesn't know much about pigs. Horses, geese, and many other animals don't know when to stop eating. But pigs seldom overeat.

Pigs

Many farm animals like to stay in big groups but not pigs. A pig enjoys going off by itself. There is only one time when pigs huddle together and that's on a cold winter night.

Barn Owls

Farm cats are good at
catching rats and mice,
but barn owls are even better.
That's the reason farmers like to have
owls living in the rafters of the barn.

A barn owl sleeps during the day and hunts
at night. An owl sees well in the dark. It can also
hear even the tiniest footstep. Then the owl flies
down from its perch so quietly that it surprises
its prey.

Barn Owls

Each year barn owls come back to the same place to nest. They are good parents. During the night, they feed their babies about ten meals.

A barn owl has a heart-shaped face. Its feathers are orange and brown. But it also has white feathers on its underside that flash in the moonlight.

When a barn owl calls, it doesn't hoot. It shrieks.